DOLLARS OF LOVE
WORKBOOK

By: Mikey and Elaine Hampson

© 2021. Dollars of Love LLC

All rights reserved. No part of this publication may be reproduced, distributed, or transmitted in any form or by any means, including photocopying, recording, or other electronic or mechanical methods, without the prior written permission of the author, except in the case of brief quotations embodied in critical reviews and certain other noncommercial uses permitted by copyright law.

Dollars of Love Workbook

Paperback ISBN: 978-1-7379934-1-4

Digital ISBN: 978-1-7379934-3-8

Hello, this is Mikey and Elaine Hampson, parents to two wonderful boys and the founders of

Dollars of Love. We wanted to tell each of you how proud we are of you for opening this book and taking the first step toward changing how the youth of today view the meaning of becoming rich.

In this notebook, you will find everything you need to create an environment in your household, classroom, ball field — or anywhere for that matter — to empower young people to pursue love and good deeds first and, through first-hand experiences, teach them the power and concept of "when we give, we receive."

The birth of Dollars of Love occurred one sunny Florida afternoon when Elaine and I were profoundly moved by the verse Luke 12:34: "For where your treasure is there your heart will be also." It challenged us to really evaluate ourselves as parents in what we were teaching our children to focus on and what they should treasure.

From the time we are born, society slams down our throats that children need to pursue accolades and financial success; we are taught that these are life's most important treasures. Children start school, where good grades are treasured and winning awards are the focal point for anything they do, and they treasure these trophies.

Our children are taught that good grades will lead to good colleges, and this, in turn, will result in a high-paying job where we can buy lots of things. To make matters worse, we make children perform chores for money so that they can buy things they treasure.

What sort of pathways in their brains are we creating at such a young age? In our opinion, these pathways lead to selfishness instead of selflessness. It also hinders the pursuit of their higher calling, instead taught to suppress it to focus on society's harmful, generalized concept of treasure.

We, as parents, decided that we did not want our children to grow up idolizing the treasures society tells us we need. They will have plenty of time to work and make money, but in our children's formidable years, we decided it was necessary to provide them with a foundation for pursuing love, kindness, and good deeds.

Thus, the birth of Dollars of Love — a currency available to all walks of life, regardless of socioeconomic status. Dollars of Love is the most powerful kind of currency because it is earned through performing good deeds and actions of love.

So, what, exactly, is a dollar of love? It is what your kids receive when they perform good deeds. At the end of the day, they will reflect upon each dollar of love earned and write on the back of it how it made them feel. At the end of the week, they can turn their dollars of love in for a prize.

In the beginning, the prizes will reinforce their positive behavior, but as the weeks progress, the children will realize that the action of Love earning them the dollar of Love made them feel better than any prize they were awarded. This creates a pathway where it becomes second nature for the child to perform a good deed. It becomes a part of who they are.

We also inadvertently came across the concept of saving the dollars of Love and trading them for rewards of various sizes. This taught our children patience and fiscal responsibility, which are important later in life.

So, how do you start the Dollars of Love program?

► Step 1: Read the children's book, Dollars of Love.

It is a story where two brothers, Bryson and Brady, go on an adventure.

They follow a treasure map and make the whole world beautiful, earning as many dollars of Love as possible.

This is a powerful story that teaches children the concept: when we give, we receive. This will motivate the child, making them want to earn dollars of Love for themselves.

► Step 2: Talk to the child about the importance of performing actions of Love and kindness.

Work to educate them on how performing good deeds makes others, as well as ourselves, feel good. Give them examples of your personal life.

► Step 3: Have the child draw on each page, showing how they will help someone in the place we listed.

For example, how will they earn dollars of Love today in school? The child could draw themselves helping a student sitting alone. They could also draw themselves picking up trash from the tables and throwing it away for the teacher.

The notebook will include different ideas/tips for students to get started.

▶ Step 4: Cut out dollars of love from the back of the book.

Have them ready for the night of reflection before bedtime.

▶ Step 5: Talk about the good deeds of the day.

Write down how it made the child feel, then have them deposit the dollars of love into a piggy bank. The piggy bank can be anything that keeps the dollars of love safe.

▶ Step 6: Reread all the dollars of love

At the end of the week, reread all the dollars of love the child earned.

Make sure you praise the child, then use a prize key you created to pick a reward.

▶ Step 7: Go out and earn dollars of love!

Take part in the activities with the children - we are never too old to become rich with dollars of love!

We taught our kids that the bigger the deed, the more dollars of love they can earn for that deed.

Below, we have provided some examples of deeds your children can do to earn their dollars of love. God bless you.

How to earn dollars of love...

▶...At breakfast: ☆

Clean up all the plates.

Surprise someone with a glass of their favorite juice.

Tell someone how great they look.

Help a parent or guardian make breakfast.

▶...In class: ☆

Make friends with a student who is sitting alone.

Clean up the trash in the classroom for the teacher.

Help a student who does not understand something.

Remind a student how great they are.

Thank your teacher for their hard work by writing them a letter.

▶...At lunch: ☆

Share your food with a student who does not have any.

Help the janitor pick up the lunch trays.

Thank the lunch person and tell them that the food is great.

Include a student who is sitting alone.

Hold the door for someone.

▶ At home: ☆

Pick a flower for a loved one.

Help clean up the yard.

Say how much you appreciate a loved one by surprising them with a kind note.

Make care packages for the homeless.

Help put the groceries away.

Provide lemonade for the garbagemen.

Help an elderly person by washing their car.

Volunteer at a group home for the elderly.

Thank a veteran for their service.

Join a group that does random acts of kindness.

▶...In your room: ☆

Put away your toys and gadgets.

Make your bed.

Fold and hang up your clothes.

▶...Before bed: ☆

Help your sibling get ready for bed.

Give thanks to God.

How else can you earn dollars of Love today?

Write down some ideas here:

_____
_____
_____
_____
_____
_____
_____
_____
_____
_____
_____
_____
_____
_____
_____
_____
_____
_____
_____
_____
_____

How to earn Dollars of Love at breakfast:

- Clean up all the plates.
- Surprise someone with a glass of their favorite juice.
- Tell someone how great they look.
- Help a parent or guardian make breakfast.

How can you earn dollars of love at breakfast?

Draw your good deed.

2

How to earn Dollars of Love in class:

- Make friends with a student who is sitting alone.
- Clean up the trash in the classroom for the teacher.
- Help a student who does not understand something.
- Remind a student how great they are.
- Thank your teacher for their hard work by writing them a letter.

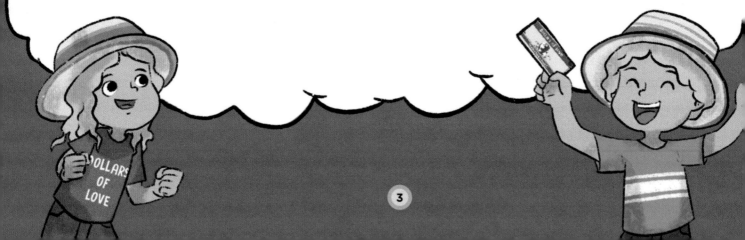

How can you earn dollars of love in class?

How can you earn dollars of Love in class?

Draw your good deed.

How to earn Dollars of Love at Lunch:

• Share your food with a student who does not have any.
• Help the janitor pick up the lunch trays.
• Thank the lunch person and tell them that the food is great.
• Include a student who is sitting alone.
• Hold the door for someone.

How can you earn dollars of love at lunch?

Draw your good deed.

How to earn Dollars of Love at home:

- Pick a flower for a loved one.
- Help clean up the yard.
- Say how much you appreciate a loved one by surprising them with a kind note.
- Make care packages for the homeless.
- Help put the groceries away.
- Provide lemonade for the garbagemen.
- Help an elderly person by washing their car.
- Volunteer at a group home for the elderly.
- Thank a veteran for their service.
- Join a group that does random acts of kindness.

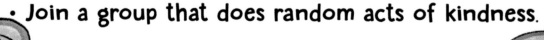

How can you earn dollars of love at home?

Draw your good deed.

How to earn Dollars of Love in your room:

- Put away your toys and gadgets.
- Make your bed.
- Fold and hang up your clothes.

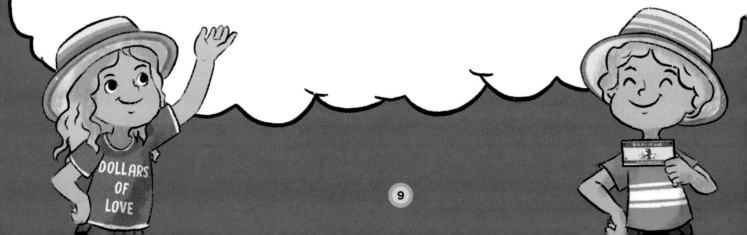

How can you earn dollars of love in your room?

Draw your good deed.

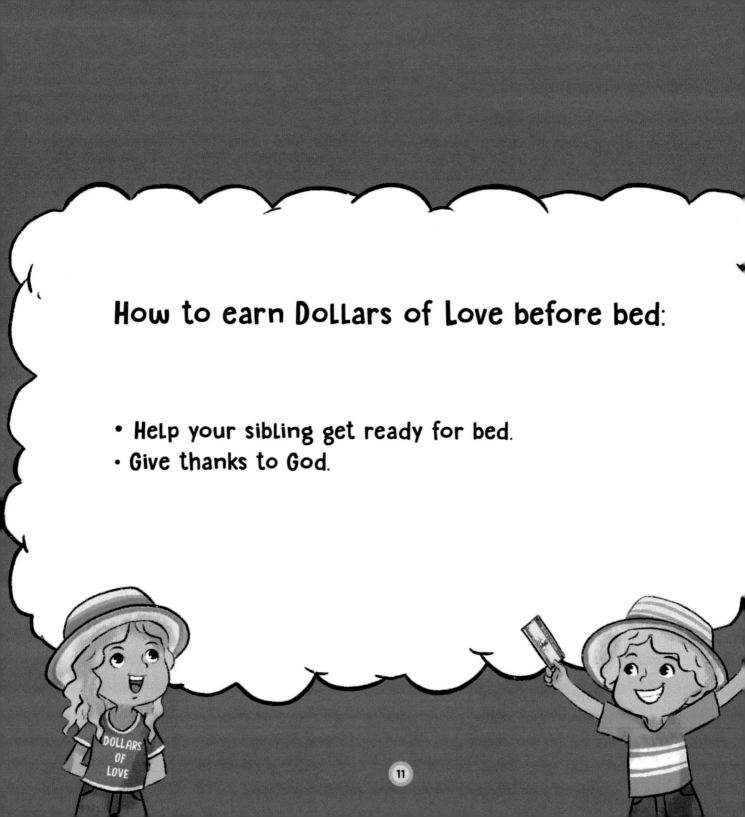

How to earn Dollars of Love before bed:

- Help your sibling get ready for bed.
- Give thanks to God.

How can you earn dollars of love before bed?

Draw your good deed.